# collected winter recipes

Kristin Hove

**hardie grant** books

MELBOURNE · LONDON

First published in 2011 by Hardie Grant Books

Hardie Grant Books (London)
Dudley House, North Suite
34–35 Southampton Street
London WC2E 7HF
www.hardiegrant.co.uk

Hardie Grant Books (Melbourne)
Ground Floor, Building 1
658 Church Street
Melbourne, VIC 3121
www.hardiegrant.com.au

British Library Cataloguing-in-Publication Data. A catalogue record
for this book is available from the British Library.

ISBN 978-1742702230

Design by Marit Hove
Photography by Kristin Hove
www.kristinhove.com
Colour reproduction by MDP
Printed and bound in China by 1010

10 9 8 7 6 5 4 3 2 1

Friends and family influence us in many ways. They make us push our boundaries, allow us to be creative, are supportive and, most of all, they inspire us.

I believe that, if we keep on being curious, adventurous and open towards each other, we can grow and achieve so much more than on our own.

This book is a result of friends' warmth and support, my family's advice, input, and a desire to create something in dedication to them all.

Growing up in Norway I learned from a young age to embrace the cold, dark wintertimes and light them up with candles, comfort food, hot drinks and warming desserts. We would gather inside to play board games and cook and bake together. The smell of cloves, cinnamon and hot chocolate would never be far away.

This book is dedicated to time spent with your closest friends and family, whether it's cooking a meal together, laughing, arguing, learning from each other, baking or swapping stories.

# contributors

### Lorraine Elliott from Australia
www.notquitenigella.com
Lorraine loves eating out in Sydney. Her recipes are inspired by the many restaurants that she visits. She likes to cook unusual, new things from all over the world.

### Eva from Norway
Eva has been kind enough to let me borrow some of her treasured collection of old Norwegian kitchenware to use as props. It has been so much fun being able to photograph food using her lovely colourful plates and pots.

### Trine from Norway
www.trinesmatblogg.no
Trine is a master when it comes to simple, tasty everyday recipes. Perfect for families on the go who still appreciate sharing a healthy meal after work and school.

### Seamus from Australia
A great improviser in the kitchen, Seamus makes the best seafood dishes, inspired by sunny Wollongong, where he was born and bred.

### Cecilie from Norway
www.lekkermunn.com
Cecilie grew up in Norway where a French neighbour served her snails, Roquefort and croissants. This later inspired her to study in France and to continuously explore French, as well as Norwegian food.

### Aran from Basque Country
www.cannelle-vanille.blogspot.com
Aran cooks the sweetest desserts and cakes, all gluten-free. She likes cooking things that smell nice and remind her of her childhood. There is a lot of nostalgia surrounding the food she makes.

### Mum from Norway
My mum loves trying out different kinds of recipes with me. It can sometimes be a challenge finding the ingredients we need in our small hometown, but that's part of the fun.

# contributors

### Paul Løve from Norway
www.sweetpaul.typepad.com
Paul is following his heart and sweet tooth. He makes things that look good and are also very tasty! He's a creative soul and is full of great ideas for how to decorate both your house and food.

### Clotilde from France
Clotilde is a lovely French girl who likes to share her affection for granola, chocolate, French food markets and restaurants.

### Line from Norway
Line's recipes are well planned, just like her wholemeal breakfast waffles, which are designed to give you enough energy for the rest of the day.

### Anders from Norway
A sport fanatic who likes spending time outdoors. His recipes often reflect his healthy lifestyle.

### Nastasja from Greece
Growing up in the Greek community means Nastaja knows the pleasure of cooking and sharing a meal with others. Her recipes have been in the family for many years and there is often a tradition behind them.

### Morten from Norway
Morten always has a healthy recipe to hand for when you don't have a clue what to have for dinner.

### Maria from Norway
My sister supports me with all my ideas and projects and is helpful and enthusiastic whenever I need an extra hand.

# contributors

### Arnstein from Norway
Arnstein tries out all the recipes I make, reads what I write and is generally the clever one with the wise words.

### Dad from Norway
Dad loves experimenting with different spices and sauces. When I was a kid he normally cooked the meals during the week. Potatoes were his essential ingredient.

### Pierre from France
Pierre's love for a good French meal is very much appreciated when you are invited for dinner at his place. Not for someone on a diet but very satisfying!

### Nicole from Australia
Since the first dinner Nicole served me, I have aimed to replicate her hosting style: she effortlessly serves amazing food.

### Tom Dyer from Australia
While flat sharing in London, I often came home to Tom cooking. The kitchen would smell of root vegetables, rosemary and lamb. He used to make big pots of everything he made, which was nice for the rest of us in the apartment.

### Tom Law from England
Tom loves being experimental in the kitchen. He's not afraid of using butter, sugar and other good stuff. He always serves a good story with his dishes.

### John Fredrik from Norway
My dear brother still hasn't cooked many meals yet, but loves sweet drinks and smoothies. One day, when he moves out of home, I'm sure he will also cook up some great dishes.

8 collected

# contributors

### Kate from Australia
My foodie friend who has written her own fantastic cook book and writes about food all day long. While living in Sydney, we used to explore the latest and greatest restaurants together.

### Stine from Norway
Stine and I used to live together when she was a student. Now, six years later, she impresses me with her newfound skills in the kitchen.

### Hanna from Norway
Hanna introduced me to a vegetarian way of eating and the food store, The Grain Shop, in London. The Grain Shop serves vegetarian, organic food. There was normally a queue, but it was always worth the wait.

### Maren from Norway
Entertaining guests can easily distract Maren from cooking, but her boyfriend Seamus is always happy to step up and help out whenever something is cooking in the oven or being fried in a pan.

### Johanna from Sweden
Johanna cooks from her heart, and is always creative. She won't cook if she isn't inspired.

### Ingrid from Norway
A confectioner who can, at any time, make the simplest caramels and cookies look like the finest candy. She enjoys helping out at weddings, christenings and other festive gatherings.

### Emma from Sweden
One of the many Swedes living outside of Sweden, Emma tries to hold on to the traditions that she brought with her from home, cooking healthy and warming dishes during winter months.

# contributors

### Sonja from Canada
Sonja is French-Canadian and makes some great meals. She's not afraid of putting the time or the best raw ingredients into them.

### Anette from Norway
Anette taught me to love traditional Norwegian dishes. She normally knows the recipes by heart.

### Grandma from Norway
I'll always remember Grandma's cookie jars, kept in the basement. Around Christmastime they were filled with the traditional seven different types of cookies.

### Sindre from Norway
Arnstein's dad cooks like a master chef and keeps teaching me things that I didn't know about cooking.

### Elise from Norway
There is often a good story behind Elise's recipes. She likes to know where the ingredients came from and gets regular deliveries from her dad, who is a hunter and fisherman.

### Gunda from Germany
A brilliant hostess who loves the combination of food and get-togethers. You always feel welcome and well looked after at the parties she hosts with her husband Mark.

12 collected

# how to create a practical kitchen

from Seamus

For Seamus, the kitchen is a place to relax, be creative, and wind down. That's why it's important to him that his kitchen is organised and well equipped.

good basic ingredients:

oregano
rosemary
dry chilli
basil
coriander
tandoori spice mix
cajun pepper
freshly ground black pepper
sea salt
good-quality extra virgin olive oil for salads
olive oil for frying
sesame oil for Asian-style food
vegetable oil for baking
balsamic vinegar

in the cupboard:

pasta
rice
fish sauce
soy sauce
sweet soy sauce
tinned tomatoes
tomato puree
stock cubes: vegetable, chicken
   and beef

Useful tips:

Cut a lemon in half and rub on chopping boards to get rid of odours from things like fish or onions.

Thaw frozen fish in milk to help remove the frozen taste and provide a fresh flavour.

If your tomatoes are becoming too ripe, simmer them for about 3 minutes with a little garlic. Store in the freezer and use later for stews and casseroles.

# the collector

Eva Aurdal

*Eva is a collector of vintage crockery. She shares with us her reasons for storing enough cups and plates to eat from a different one each day of the year:*

I collect mostly from the 50s and 60s because that's when I grew up; it's out of nostalgia. I still find things from this time bring back forgotten memories.

This era also represents a time when things were meant to be both functional and practical. It was when women stopped being housewives and started working. Things were therefore designed to make cooking easier.

It is, of course, the aesthetic part of it I like as well. I like a clean, sharp look with strong colours and simple graphics. This is crockery made to be used, and it feels honest and real to me.

I also collect older furniture like lamps and tables. These help you create your own personal touch, mixing different styles.

I think it's important to use the resources we have more carefully, and to move away from a 'use and throw' mentality. For the environment's sake we should try to reuse as much as we can.

# winter body scrubs

from Maria
fills 3 medium-sized glass jars.

sweet body scrub:
1 cup desiccated coconut
1 cup sugar
½ cup baby oil
1 teaspoon vanilla essence
1 teaspoon cinnamon

These scrubs make your skin glow in the wintertime and smell like Christmas. Maria made these last year for her friends, as a treat in the winter darkness.

salty body scrub:
1 cup sea salt
1 cup sugar
½ cup baby oil
1 tablespoon orange zest
1 tablespoon grated ginger

For each scrub, combine all the ingredients in a bowl. Use a clean jar with a lid and fill it up with the mixture. If it is too dry, add more oil. Decorate the glass jar with a gift tag, string or ribbon.

# breakfast

Start the day with a smile and
a good breakfast

# winter smoothie

from John Fredrik
serves 2

2 cups forest berries
½ cup water
2 teaspoons freshly grated ginger
1 teaspoon cardamom pods, seeds removed
1 cup milk
¼ cup oats

to serve:
a few fresh blueberries
dark chocolate, grated

During the summertime John Fredrik makes this smoothie without the oats and leaves it in the freezer for a couple of hours, until it turns to slush.

Simmer the berries, ginger, cardamom pods and water for 2 minutes. Add the milk and oats and simmer for another 3 minutes. Blend quickly.

Serve with berries and grated chocolate on top.

# pumpkin pancakes

from Elise
serves 4

2 eggs
1½ cups condensed milk
400 g pumpkin puree (peel and bake the pumpkin in chunks for an hour
    before making the puree)
250 g flour
3 tablespoons brown sugar
1 teaspoon cardamom pods, seeds removed, ready to use
1 teaspoon cinnamon
1 teaspoon nutmeg
1 teaspoon ground cloves
1 teaspoon baking powder
½ teaspoon baking soda
¼ teaspoon salt
2 tablespoons butter, for frying

Elise loves this vegetable and uses it in cakes, soups and dinners. It makes these pancakes moist and filling.

to serve:
100 g pecan nuts
⅓ cup maple syrup

Beat the eggs and add all the other ingredients. Stir well, then let the batter rest for half an hour. Melt the butter in a frying pan. Dollop spoonfuls of the batter into the pan and cook in batches until golden. In another pan, fry the pecans until brown, then pour maple syrup over them and let the mixture boil for a couple of minutes.

Pour nuts and syrup over the pancakes before serving.

# breakfast waffles

from Line
serves 4

3 eggs
2 cups milk
½ cup vegetable oil
⅔ cup flour
⅔ cup oatmeal
⅔ cup wholemeal flour
vegetable oil for frying

to serve:
4 teaspoons honey
1 handful of hazelnuts, chopped
½ cup fresh blueberries

Line's version of traditional waffles. Same pleasure, just a bit more healthy.

Beat the eggs lightly before adding the rest of the ingredients. Let them stand for 30 minutes before frying them on a lightly oiled waffle iron. Leave them in the waffle iron until they turn golden.

Serve with honey, hazelnuts and blueberries.

# macadamia maple granola

from Clotilde
serves 6

2 tablespoons butter
6 tablespoons maple syrup
1 cup porridge oats
½ teaspoon fine sea salt
⅔ cup macadamia nuts, roughly chopped
1 teaspoon freshly grated lime zest

This is Clothilde's perfect breakfast, which will leave the house smelling of roasted lime and maple syrup.

Preheat the oven to 180°C.

Line a rimmed baking sheet with greaseproof paper. Combine the butter and maple syrup in a small saucepan and set on a medium heat until the butter is melted, but not boiling. Remove from heat.

Combine the oats, salt, macadamia nuts and lime zest in a medium-sized mixing bowl. Pour in the butter and maple syrup mixture, and stir to combine. Spread onto the prepared baking sheet, and slip into the oven for 12 minutes, or until golden. Stir the mixture once or twice as it bakes. Remove from the oven and let cool. Store in an airtight container.

Serve with vanilla yogurt or milk.

# healthy pancakes

from Morten
serves 3

3 eggs
1¼ cups oats
1¼ cups flour
1 cup cottage cheese
1¼ cups milk or soya milk
2 teaspoons vegetable oil
1 teaspoon salt
3 tablespoons butter for frying

Morten's advice is to not make the pancakes too big.

to serve:
½ cup cottage cheese
3 tablespoons jam

Gently beat the eggs. Add the other ingredients and combine well. Allow to rest for 30 minutes.

Heat 1 teaspoon of butter in a frying pan over a medium heat. When hot, add a dollop of batter and cook for a couple of minutes each side, until golden.

Serve with cottage cheese and jam or honey, apples and nuts.

# banana and walnut bread

from Maren
makes 2 loaves

3 eggs
2 cups sugar
2 bananas
3 cups flour
1 teaspoon cardamom pods,
    seeds removed ready for use
2 teaspoons baking soda
2 teaspoons vanilla sugar
1 teaspoon bicarbonate of soda
1 handful of chopped walnuts
8 tablespoons milk
1 cup melted butter

to serve:
sliced banana

While living in Sydney, Maren and I developed a love for this tasty loaf. Nothing is better than a good catch-up over a slice of banana bread and a soya latte.

Preheat the oven to 180°C. Grease two loaf tins and line with baking paper.

Beat the eggs and sugar until fluffy. Mash the bananas and add to the mixture. Add all the dry ingredients and mix well before adding the walnuts, milk and then melted butter. Stir thoroughly and transfer into the loaf tins. Bake for 45 minutes or until springy to the touch.

Serve with sliced banana.

# cinnamon fruit bread

from Kristin
makes 3 loaves

125 g butter
2 cups milk
50 g fresh yeast or 1 sachet dry yeast
125 g sugar
1 teaspoon cardamom pods,
    seeds removed ready for use
1 teaspoon cinnamon
1 teaspoon nutmeg
900 g flour
75 g raisins
75 g dried apricots, chopped
2 eggs, lightly beaten

> Perfect for a long Sunday breakfast. Wrap your loaf in baking paper, then tie it up with string, and you'll have a nice treat to give away.

Melt the butter over a medium heat and add the milk. Let the mixture cool slightly before dissolving the yeast in the liquid. When the yeast is blended, add the sugar, spices and flour. Use a food processor to combine or knead for as long as you can, a minimum of 10 minutes. Cover the bowl with clingfilm and leave to rise overnight.

Preheat the oven to 180°C. Grease 3 loaf tins and line them with baking paper.

Add the raisins and apricots to the dough and knead briefly. Divide the dough into three parts and roll them into rounds. Let stand for another 40 minutes under a tea towel before brushing them lightly with egg. Bake for 45 minutes, or until springy to the touch.

Serve on its own or with butter and jam.

# soups

just what you need on a cold day

# chunky tomato soup

from Johanna
serves 3

1 tablespoon olive oil
1 teaspoon red chilli paste
½ onion, chopped
2 garlic cloves, crushed
2 x 390 g tins of chopped tomatoes
3 teaspoons crème fraiche
a handful of fresh basil leaves

Johanna created this from leftovers in the fridge. It works really well, and has been cooked many times.

Warm the oil in a frying pan with the chilli paste. Add the onions and garlic and simmer for a few minutes until the onions are clear. Add the tomatoes and simmer for 10 minutes.

Serve with a dollop of crème fraiche and garnish with some basil leaves.

# vietnamese pho soup

from Tom Dyer
serves 4

1½ litres good-quality beef stock
10 star anise
1 cinnamon stick
5 cardamom pods, seeds removed, ready for use
6 cloves
2 thumb-sized pieces of ginger, cut in half lengthwise and lightly bruised in a
   pestle and mortar
2 shallots
375 g flat rice noodles
1 spring onion, sliced finely
200 g beef fillet, cut paper-thin
1 cup bean sprouts
1 cup Thai basil
2 small red chillies, sliced
fish sauce, to taste
4 lime wedges, to serve

> Tom was inspired by the many great street kitchens in Asia to make this soup. I love the cinnamon and the freshness of it.

Place the stock, star anise, cinnamon, cardamom, cloves, ginger and shallots in a saucepan over a high heat and bring to the boil. Reduce the heat to low and simmer for 30 minutes. Remove spices and shallots from stock. Cook the noodles according to packet instructions. Drain and divide between serving bowls.

Top the noodles with the spring onion, beef, bean sprouts, Thai basil and chilli and pour over the stock. The stock will cook the raw fillet steaks. To serve, add the fish sauce and a squeeze of lime juice.

# dad's fish soup

from Dad
serves 6

2 shallots, finely chopped
500 g fresh mussels, rinsed and cleaned
⅓ cup white wine
5 cups fish stock
2 carrots, finely sliced
1 spring onion, finely sliced
1 kg fish (salmon, cod, snapper etc.), cut into small cubes
⅔ cup double cream
salt and pepper
100 g peeled raw prawns
2 tablespoons olive oil, for frying

to serve:
parsley, chopped

My dad makes a big batch of this soup when we have guests over and serves it as an evening snack. It can be reheated the day after as well.

In a heavy-bottomed saucepan, fry the shallots until soft. Add the mussels for 30 seconds. Next, add the white wine and cook, covered, for 2 minutes. Remove the mussels and add the fish stock and vegetables. Simmer for 20 minutes before you add the fish. Leave on a low heat for 5 minutes. Pour in the cream and season with salt and pepper. Put the mussels back into the soup with the prawns for a few minutes, until cooked through.

Garnish with parsley before serving.

# french onion soup

from Nicole
serves 4

50 g butter
750 g brown onions
⅓ cup plain flour
2 litres beef stock
1 cup white wine
1 bay leaf
2 thyme sprigs
croutons
Gruyère cheese

If you want to add a special festive flavour to this soup, do what Nicole does and add a couple of tablespoons of cognac while frying the onions.

In a large saucepan, melt the butter and sauté the onions until they are golden brown and starting to caramelise. Add the flour and stir continuously for 1 minute. Gradually add the beef stock and wine. Bring to the boil, add the herbs and simmer for 25 minutes.

Spoon into ovenproof bowls, and top with croutons and cheese. Grill until the cheese is brown and serve.

# chicken soup

from Seamus
serves 6

3 litres water
1 cooked chicken
2 chicken stock cubes
1 vegetable stock cube
3 cloves garlic, finely chopped
1 small chilli, deseeded and finely chopped
8 peppercorns, crushed

Seamus's current choice of vegetables:
2 carrots, diced
2 onions, diced
3 potatoes
½ broccoli, broken into florets
10 sliced mushrooms
salt and pepper to season

Seamus uses this stock as a base for many soups, changing the vegetables from time to time, depending on what's in the fridge or in season. It's a great way of using leftover vegetables.

In a large saucepan, dissolve the stock in 2 litres of boiling water.

Add the chicken, and let it simmer for 30 minutes. Remove the carcass from the stock, and strip the flesh from the bones. Put the meat back into the stock and add the garlic, chilli, pepper, vegetables and the rest of the water. Let it simmer for another hour.

Season to taste and serve with crusty bread.

# dinner

welcome to the table

# aud's meat cakes

from Anette
serves 4

500 g minced beef
½ onion, finely chopped
¼ cup water
2 tablespoons potato flour
3 teaspoons pepper
2 teaspoons salt
2 tablespoons butter, for frying

for the gravy:
2 tablespoons butter
3 tablespoons flour
2 cups beef stock

> The key to this recipe is a lot of love. Anette makes these from the memory of how her mum used to make them. She sometimes serves them with macaroni stew.

Mix the minced beef with the onion, water, potato flour, salt and pepper. Use a spoon to measure the meat cakes – each portion should be 2 tablespoons of mixture. Dip the spoon in cold water and shape each meat cake. Place in a frying pan and fry on both sides until brown.

Use the same frying pan, without washing it, to make the gravy. Add the rest of the butter and flour and stir with a wooden spoon until smooth. Then add the beef stock and transfer to a casserole dish with the meat cakes. Simmer for 10 minutes.

Serve with lingonberry jam and boiled potatoes.

# perfect picnic quiche

from Lorraine
serves 4

filling:
½ cup Cheddar, grated
200 g Prosciutto
3 spring onions, finely sliced
2 tablespoons parsley
2 tablespoons plain flour
1 tablespoon mayonnaise
5 large eggs
1–1¼ cups milk

handful of cherry tomatoes, halved
75 g feta, torn into small pieces
salt and pepper, to season

pastry:
200 g cream cheese
125 g cold butter
1–1¼ cups plain flour

Preheat the oven to 220°C.

> Lorraine's choice for an outdoor meal.
> This quiche is easy to transport and is
> perfect for sharing with friends.

Place a baking tray in the oven to preheat. To make the pastry, chop the cream cheese and place it in a microwave-proof jug. Cover and microwave for 1–2 minutes until soft. Working quickly, grate the chilled butter, add to the cream cheese and mix well. Stir in 1 cup of flour. If the dough is too soft, add the extra flour. Tip into a flan tin and lightly dust with flour, then press out over the base and sides.

Place all filling ingredients, except for the feta and cherry tomatoes, into a bowl. Beat until combined and pour into the pastry case. Scatter the feta and cherry tomatoes over the top and push down until they are half submerged in the egg mixture. Season with salt and pepper. Bake for 10 minutes at 220°C, then reduce the temperature to 180°C and bake for a further 20 minutes until golden and firm.

Let stand for 10 minutes before serving.

# indian chickpea stew

from Cecilie
serves 2

1 tin chickpeas
1 onion, finely chopped
1 tablespoon butter, for frying
7 tomatoes, chopped
2 tablespoons garam masala
1 handful of cashew nuts
2 tablespoons natural yogurt

A midweek meal by Cecilie. Just spicy enough, and takes no time to make.

to serve:
1 cup cooked rice

Rinse and drain the chickpeas. Fry the onion in butter until golden. Add the chickpeas and tomatoes and simmer for 15 minutes. Add 2 tablespoons of curry paste and stir well. Simmer for 2 more minutes.

Serve with cashew nuts and 1 tablespoon of natural yogurt on a bed of rice.

# apple schnapps gravlax

from Kate

½ bunch dill, finely chopped
2 tablespoons white sugar
2 tablespoons good quality sea salt
2 tablespoons apple schnapps
300 g fillet of salmon, skin on

to serve:
rye bread, mustard and extra dill

> Kate made the first gravlax that I actually liked. It might have something to do with me having matured enough to like the taste now, but I stick to this recipe.

Combine all the ingredients, except the fish. Rub the mixture over the fish fillet, packing it onto both sides. Cover with clingfilm, ensuring the clingfilm is contained inside the dish. Refrigerate for 18–24 hours (depending on size of fillet).

Serve thinly sliced with rye bread, mustard and extra dill.

# chanterelles risotto

from Stine
serves 4

1 clove garlic, finely chopped
4 shallots, chopped
150 g risotto rice
250 g bacon, diced
1½ cups white wine
1¾ cups chicken broth
¼ cup olive oil
¾ cup cream
60 g slivered Parmesan cheese
juice and zest of half a lemon
15–20 chanterelles
salt and pepper
butter and vegetable oil for frying

> Stine makes all dishes taste and look delicious. This one is usually part of a three-course meal. Yummy!

Fry the garlic, shallots, rice and bacon for 2 minutes. Add the white wine and let the mixture simmer for a few more minutes. Pour in the chicken broth and simmer under a lid for 7 minutes, stirring occasionally.

Clean the chanterelles and fry them with 1 tablespoon vegetable oil, without stirring, on a medium heat. After 2 minutes, add 1 tablespoon butter and stir gently so both sides brown. Add half of the chanterelles to the risotto.

Add the cream to the risotto and stir for a few minutes before adding Parmesan, lemon juice and zest, then season to taste. Just before serving add the remaining chanterelles to garnish.

# a spinach dream

from Hanna
serves 4

4 cloves garlic, crushed and chopped
1 onion, finely chopped
2 tablespoons olive oil
10–12 mushrooms, sliced
1 teaspoon salt
1 teaspoon pepper
2 teaspoons oregano
1 cup cream
450 g frozen spinach
500 g wholemeal spaghetti, cooked
30 g Jarlsberg cheese, grated
30 g Parmesan cheese, grated

For a vegetarian like Hanna, spinach is an essential ingredient, being packed with iron.

Fry the garlic and onion in the olive oil until soft and golden. Add the mushrooms, spinach and spices.

Fry for a few more minutes before adding the cream, then let it simmer for a couple of minutes. Combine the spaghetti with the spinach.

Top with Parmesan and Jarlsberg just before serving.

# pasta with roquefort and walnuts

from Cecilie
serves 4

A dish Cecilie learned to make when she was a student in France. It's quick, cheap and tasty, which gives you more time to study or drink rosé wine!

400 g penne pasta
150 g Roquefort, or any other blue cheese
4 tablespoons crème fraiche
2 handfuls walnuts, chopped

Boil the pasta according to packet instructions. Use a fork to break up the Roquefort. Warm the crème fraiche in a pan and add the Roquefort for just a few seconds. Add to the pasta while still warm, along with the chopped walnuts.

Enjoy with a slice of cold cuts, bread, or on its own.

# baked cod with feta and cherry tomatoes

from Trine
serves 3

1 red onion, sliced
2 tablespoons olive oil
200 g spinach
100 g feta, cut into cubes
10 cherry tomatoes, sliced in half
500 g cod fillets
juice of ½ lemon

> Trine uses tomatoes in quite a few of her recipes – they look good and add a freshness to the dish. You can make this recipe with snapper, barramundi or any other white fish.

Preheat the oven to 200°C.

Fry the red onion in a pan with 1 tablespoon olive oil until clear. Turn the heat down and add the spinach. Fry for a few more minutes, then place onion and spinach in a baking dish.

Top the spinach with feta and cherry tomatoes. Place the cod fillets on top and drizzle over lemon juice, the rest of the olive oil and season to taste. Bake for about 15 minutes.

Serve with rice or potatoes.

# baked salmon á la kleven

from Maren
serves 4

half a salmon side (approx 800 g)
3 tablespoons green pesto
2 teaspoons fresh thyme
1 teaspoon paprika
⅔ cup crème fraiche
salt and pepper to season

A typical Sunday dinner with the Kleven family. It's a 'no hassle' recipe that allows plenty of time to relax.

Preheat the oven to 180°C.

On a piece of oiled aluminum foil, place the salmon, skin side down. Combine pesto, spices and crème fraiche and pour over the fish. Wrap foil tightly around the salmon and bake in the oven for 25 minutes.

Serve with a green salad and potatoes.

# maple syrup and passion fruit roasted chicken

from Paul
serves 6

1 large chicken
salt and pepper
1 kg small potatoes
8 shallots, peeled and cut in half
10 cloves of garlic, peeled
2 large carrots, diced
10 sage leaves
½ cup maple syrup
½ cup passion fruit pulp
3 tablespoons apricot jam

for the sauce:
1 cup chicken dripping
½ vegetable stock cube
½ cup water
½ cup cream

Paul promises that people will clear their plates with this sauce. Serve it with some bread so guests can mop up every last bit.

Preheat the oven to 220°C.

Rub the chicken with salt and pepper. Place all the vegetables and herbs in a large roasting tray and place the chicken on top. Stir together the maple syrup, passion fruit pulp and apricot jam in a bowl. Baste the chicken with the mixture.
Place the chicken in the oven and roast for about 1 ½ hours, or until the skin is golden and the juices run clear when pierced, basting the chicken every 15 minutes with the maple mixture. Then take the chicken out and pour the chicken dripping into a saucepan. Add the vegetable stock cube and water, and bring to a boil. Let the sauce simmer until reduced and add cream. Cook for 2 minutes, then season to taste with salt and pepper.

Serve the chicken with the vegetables and the sauce.

# a norwegian sunday dinner

from Sindre
serves 4

500 g potatoes, peeled and diced
2 carrots, peeled and grated
1 green apple, peeled and thinly sliced
3 teaspoons natural yogurt
1 teaspoon honey
1 tablespoon currants
⅓ cup cream
3 tablespoons olive oil
4 teaspoons pesto
600 g cod filets
lemon pepper, to season

Sindre is a fish specialist and this recipe is one of his easy and quick-to-prepare Sunday meals. You can try it with any white fish.

Boil the potatoes for about 10 minutes, or until tender. Meanwhile, combine the carrots and apples with the yogurt, honey and currants. Place in the fridge until ready to serve.

When the potatoes are ready, mash them with cream, a tablespoon of olive oil and pesto until fluffy.

Season the cod with lemon pepper and fry with the remaining olive oil for a few minutes on each side. Serve immediately with the pesto mash and carrot and apple salad.

# coq au vin

from Pierre
serves 8

2 medium-sized chickens cut into 8 pieces each
1 bottle red wine
2 bay leaves
2 sprigs fresh thyme
salt and pepper
60 g butter
250 g bacon, chopped
20 g shallots
250 g button mushrooms
¼ cup plain flour
1 litre chicken stock
½ cup brandy
2 teaspoons tomato puree
1½ tablespoons chopped parsley

This was one of the first French dishes I got served by Pierre. Eating it will always bring back good memories.

Put the chicken into a bowl with the wine, bay leaves, thyme and some salt and pepper. Marinate overnight. Drain the chicken, reserve the marinade. Melt 15 grams of the butter, fry the bacon, then remove from pan. Melt another 15 grams of the butter, fry the shallots until soft, and remove from pan. Do the same with the mushrooms, then the chicken.

While the chicken is in the pan, stir in the flour, cook for 1 minute, then remove the chicken and deglaze the pan with brandy. Put the cooked ingredients back into the pan, along with the marinade, chicken stock and tomato puree. Simmer for 45 minutes until the chicken is cooked through. Garnish with parsley.

# fish curry

from Arnstein
serves 4

> Arnstein picked up this recipe when we were travelling in Thailand. After some experimenting, he has now found the right amount of chilli for it. Feel free to add some more if you can handle it.

16–20 small potatoes, cut in half
2 tablespoons vegetable oil
2 tablespoons yellow curry paste
1 cup chicken stock
2 cans of 400 ml coconut cream
2 fresh kaffir limes, stem removed and finely sliced
1 cup sweet basil, plus extra to garnish
1 chilli, thinly sliced
4 teaspoons fish sauce
1 teaspoon sugar
½ teaspoon white pepper
700 g salmon, cut into bite-sized pieces

Boil the potatoes for 15–20 minutes.

Heat a wok or frying pan over a medium heat and add the oil. Add the curry paste and stock and simmer for 2 minutes. Add the coconut cream, limes, basil and chilli. Stir-fry for 1 minute. Add the fish sauce, sugar, white pepper and the fish. Cook for 2 minutes, or until fish is cooked through, stirring occasionally. Lastly, add the boiled potatoes to the curry.

Serve with rice.

# baccalà

from Mum
serves 4

700 g soaked baccalà
600 g potatoes, peeled and thinly sliced
½ cup olive oil
4 onions, chopped
2 tablespoons tomato puree
400 g tinned tomatoes
200 g preserved peppers in oil
½ teaspoon cayenne pepper

This is one of the meals I always ask my mum to cook when I go home. On the west coast in Norway we claim this as our own dish, but it originally came from Portugal.

Rinse the salt from the baccalà and soak it in water for at least 12 hours, changing the water two or three times.

Once soaked, remove skin and bones from the fish and cut it into bite-sized pieces. Layer all the ingredients in the pan and let it cook for about 45 minutes.

Serve with bread.

# bolognaise à la québécoise

from Sonia
serves 8-10

4 carrots
3 celery stalks
2 courgettes
1 medium onion
2 garlic cloves
1 kg minced beef
a handful of white button mushrooms, sliced
725 ml tomato sauce
300 ml tomato puree
540 ml chopped tomatoes
2 tablespoons soy sauce
2 tablespoons Worcestershire sauce
½ cup apple cider vinegar
¾ cup ketchup (organic, please!)
1 teaspoon each of coriander, cardamom seeds, thyme, oregano
    and cumin
2 bay leaves
2 chopped red chillis

to serve:
pasta and fresh basil leaves, torn

Dice all the vegetables, except the mushrooms. Sauté with the garlic for a few minutes, then add the mince. Brown the mince, then add the mushrooms and remaining ingredients. Simmer for an hour and half, if not longer, stirring every 20 minutes. Serve on the pasta, and top with the basil leaves.

> Sonia normally cooks a big batch of this dish, and with the leftovers she makes individual portions that she freezes and reheats on lazy or busy days.

# dessert

something sweet

# grandpa's fruit soup

from Elise
serves 4

4 tablespoons barley
1 litre water
10 dried apricots
10 prunes
4 tablespoons raisins
2 tablespoons sugar

Elise's grandpa used to make a big pot of this soup and serve it for dessert for the whole week. Originally he didn't put sugar in it, but most people will prefer slightly sweeter.

to serve:
ice cream and a sprinkle of cinnamon

Soak the barley in water overnight.

Boil the water and barley. Remove the foam from the surface and add dried fruit. Let the soup simmer for about 30 minutes.

Serve while warm with a scoop of ice cream and a sprinkle of cinnamon.

# prune and yogurt cocktail with chocolate

from Paul
serves 4

½ cup prunes
1 teaspoon sugar
¼ vanilla pod, just the seeds
2 tablespoons boiling water
1 cup plain yogurt
2 teaspoons grated dark chocolate

Prunes are often associated with something you would find in your grandparents' fridge. This dessert is so good – 'cool' to serve to friends, but still very grandma-friendly. And it only takes a few minutes to make.

Place the prunes, sugar, vanilla seeds and water in a blender and whiz until smooth. Spoon the mixture into 4 glasses.

Top with yogurt and chocolate.

# apple crumble

from Nicole

filling:
4 granny smith apples, diced
2 teaspoons brown sugar
1 cinnamon stick
1 cup of water
3 sheets filo pastry, thawed
3 tablespoons melted butter

crumble:
¼ cup plain flour
¼ cup sugar
100 g butter
sprinkle of cinnamon
handful chopped pecans

> Crumbles have lately become my favourite desserts. This is Nicole's fancy version of it, which looks great at dinner parties.

Preheat the oven to 180°C.

In a saucepan combine the apples, brown sugar, cinnamon stick and water. Gently simmer until the apple is soft, which should take about 10 minutes. Drain any excess liquid and set aside.

Brush 4 muffin cups with melted butter. Separate the filo pastry sheets and gently brush each pastry sheet with melted butter, then stack on top of one another. Cut the sheet into quarters and gently place in muffin cups. Set aside.

Combine the flour, sugar, butter and cinnamon and rub together with your fingers until the mixture resembles breadcrumbs, then add the pecans. Assemble by filling the filo cups with apple mixture, top with crumble and bake for 15–20 minutes or until golden.

Serve with ice cream.

# gingerbread cake

from Tom
makes about 12 nice hunks

100 g butter
100 g light muscovado sugar / soft brown sugar
150 g Tate & Lyle black treacle
150 g Tate & Lyle golden syrup
250 g plain flour
1 teaspoon bicarbonate of soda
thumb-sized piece of peeled fresh ginger,
    finely grated
1 teaspoon mixed spice, cinnamon or nutmeg,
    or all 3
2 eggs, beaten
150 g crystallised stem ginger, finely chopped

icing:
125 g butter at room
    temperature
225 g icing sugar, sifted
30 ml milk
1 teaspoon cinnamon

Tom loves personalising his recipes. With this one he simply chucked in a pile of freshly grated ginger. If your love for ginger is as big as his, you should give it a go. It's very nice indeed!

Preheat the oven to 170°C. Grease a deep, 20-cm round cake tin and line with baking paper.

Combine the butter, sugar, treacle and golden syrup in a big pan and stir until melted. Remove from the heat. Sift the flour and bicarbonate of soda in a large bowl, then add the grated ginger, spices and chopped ginger. Stir well and add the eggs. Stir again, then pour into the prepared cake tin. Cook for 35–40 minutes or until firm.

To make the icing, beat the butter for 2 minutes until light and fluffy, add the icing sugar bit by bit, then add the milk until smooth. Spread onto the cooled cake and finish with a dusting of cinnamon.

# chai-infused cinnamon cake

from Nastassja

3 chai-infused black tea bags
5–6 very ripe bananas
4 cups flour
2 teaspoons baking powder
1 teaspoon salt
1 teaspoon cinnamon
1 teaspoon nutmeg
250 g unsalted butter
½ cup brown sugar
4 eggs, beaten
2 tablespoons vanilla essence

> Nastassja's cinnamon heaven. As cinnamon is my favourite spice, I need say no more.

icing:
250 g cream cheese, softened
125 g butter, at room temperature
½ cup icing sugar
2 teaspoons cinnamon
2 teaspoons vanilla essence
3 teaspoons cooled chai tea

Preheat the oven to 180°C. Grease a deep, 20-cm round cake tin and line with baking paper.

Put 3 tea bags in a mug and add boiling water to cover. Infuse and allow to cool. Mash the bananas using a fork. In a bowl sift the flour, baking powder, salt, cinnamon and nutmeg. In another bowl, blend the butter and sugar until fluffy. Then stir in the eggs, vanilla essence and mashed bananas, and about 8–10 tablespoons of cooled tea. Combine with the dry mixture and stir until fully mixed. Spoon into the tin and cook for about 1 hour and 15 minutes (cake). If making cupcakes, use cupcake cases and bake for just 15 minutes.

To make the icing, beat the cream cheese and butter together in a bowl, then slowly add the other ingredients. Spread onto the cooled cake.

# chocolate and courgette cake

from Clotilde
serves 12

> For Clotilde, this recipe comes quite naturally, but it does sound a tad strange. You just have to try it!

2 cups flour
½ cup unsweetened cocoa powder
1 teaspoon baking soda
½ teaspoon baking powder
½ teaspoon fine sea salt
1 cup light brown sugar
½ cup unsalted butter at room temperature or ½ cup virgin olive oil
to serve: grated courgette and icing sugar

1 teaspoon pure vanilla extract
2 tablespoons strong cooled coffee
3 large eggs
2 cups unpeeled grated courgette, from about 1½ medium courgettes
1 cup good-quality grated chocolate (minimum 70% cocoa)

Preheat the oven to 180°C. Grease a 25-cm (10-inch) round springform tin.

In a medium-sized mixing bowl, combine the flour, cocoa powder, baking soda, baking powder and salt. Beat the sugar and butter in a mixer until they go fluffy. Add the vanilla extract, coffee and eggs, mixing well between each addition. In a large mixing bowl combine the courgette, chocolate and about a third of the flour mixture, making sure the courgette strands are well coated and not clumping too much. Add the rest of the flour mixture into the batter. Mix until just combined; the batter should be thick. Fold the courgette mixture into the batter and blend with a spatula without over-mixing. Pour into the prepared cake tin and level the surface. Bake for 40–50 minutes, until a knife inserted in the centre comes out clean. Transfer onto a rack to cool for 10 minutes, run a knife around the tin to loosen, and unclasp the sides of the tin.

Serve slightly warm or at room temperature. Sprinkle with icing sugar and some freshly grated courgette.

# sweet potato, yogurt and hazelnut cake

from Aran
makes 1 loaf

160 g flour
40 g hazelnut flour
1 teaspoon sea salt
1 teaspoon baking soda
½ teaspoon cinnamon
¼ teaspoon ginger
a large pinch of freshly grated nutmeg
300 g sweet potato puree

100 g brown sugar
50 g granulated sugar
3 eggs
100 g yogurt
100 g vegetable oil
zest of half an orange
130 g hazelnuts, toasted and chopped
30 g hazelnuts, chopped for topping

> Aran makes the sweetest gluten-free desserts. You can also try this cake with pumpkin instead of sweet potatoes.

Preheat the oven to 180°C. Grease a loaf tin (23 ½ x 13 ½ x 7 cm) and line with baking paper.

In a large bowl combine the flour, hazelnut flour, salt, baking soda, cinnamon, ginger and nutmeg. In a separate bowl whisk together the sweet potato puree, brown sugar, granulated sugar, eggs, yogurt, oil and orange zest. Pour the wet ingredients over the dry and whisk until combined. It should be a runny batter. Fold in the toasted hazelnuts. Pour the batter into the tin (about ¾ of the way full) then sprinkle the top with chopped hazelnuts and bake until a skewer inserted in the centre comes out clean, which should take about 17 minutes.

# gluehwein

from Gunda
serves 10

1 tablespoon black tea leaves
8 cloves
2 cinnamon sticks
200–250 g of sugar
½ bottle of rum
2 bottles of red wine
2 oranges, cut into small pieces

A classic welcome tipple at Mark and Gunda's parties. The drink tends to get stronger during the course of the evening.

Brew the tea, then add the cloves, cinnamon sticks, sugar, rum and red wine. Keep hot, just below boiling point, for about 5 minutes.

Add the oranges and cool for a couple of hours. Warm, without boiling, before serving.

# mozart kuler

from Emma

100 g nougat
400 g marzipan
250 g dark chocolate

For a Swedish version you can also add 1 teaspoon of cognac to the marzipan before rolling them out. Emma prefers them without.

Cut the nougat block into small cubes.

Roll the marzipan into a long sausage and cut ½ cm thick slices from it. Flatten the marzipan a little and put the nougat in the middle. Roll into a little ball with the nougat inside the marzipan. Melt the chocolate in a deep bowl placed on top of a saucepan of boiling water. Using a toothpick, pick up a 'ball' and dip one side of it in the chocolate. Alternatively you can dip them all the way in, like we do!

Place on a tray until the chocolate has cooled.

# sirupsnitter

from Grandma

100 g treacle
60 g sugar
50 ml cream
60 g butter
1 egg yolk
225–250 g flour
¼ teaspoon ginger
½ teaspoon pepper
4 teaspoons baking soda
peeled almonds to decorate

My grandma is the queen of cookies. These have been made many times in her kitchen.

Preheat the oven to 180°C.

Boil the treacle, sugar and cream. Pour over the butter and stir it in. Add the egg yolk and allow it to cool. Blend the flour with the ginger and baking soda and mix it all together. When the dough is smooth, cover and place in the fridge overnight.

Divide the dough into two small parts and roll it with a rolling pin until the dough is as flat as you can get it. You can use some flour on the surface, but try to use as little as possible. Slice the dough into a rectangular shape and place it on a tray with baking paper. Lightly push an almond into the centre for decoration. Bake in the oven for 8–10 minutes.

Leave to cool on a wire rack.

# mints

from Ingrid
makes about 50

250 g icing sugar
5 g gum tragacanth
1 egg white, whisked
6 drops of peppermint oil
100 g dark chocolate

These mouthfuls of mint and chocolate are perfect after a meal. Ingrid makes them in five minutes so if you request mints she'll have them on the table before the evening is over.

Sift the icing sugar into a bowl and add the gum tragacanth and egg white.

Combine and knead well (you might need more icing sugar depending on the size of the egg you use). Make a long roll and slice into 2 cm cubes. Roll each cube and flatten a little bit.

Melt the chocolate by placing it in a small plastic lunch bag and submerging the bag in a glass of hot water. When the chocolate has melted, use scissors to cut a small hole in one of the corners. Now you can decorate the mints by drizzling them with chocolate.

Store in a cool place.

# rice pudding

from Anders
serves 4

1 cup water
100 g long-grain rice
2 ½ cups milk
½ teaspoon salt
1 cup cream
1 teaspoon vanilla sugar
to serve: red berry coulis

A very traditional Norwegian dessert, often made from leftover rice porridge with cream. A favourite dessert for Anders on Christmas Eve.

Boil the water and add the rice in a saucepan with the lid on and let it boil until all the water has been absorbed. Add the milk and simmer for about 40 minutes, stirring often. Set aside to cool for a few hours.

Whip the cream until it forms soft peaks, then add the vanilla sugar. Gently fold into the porridge.

Serve with a red berry coulis.

# double chocolate and crystallised ginger biscotti

from Aran
serves 6

150 g butter at room temperature
200 g sugar
zest of 1 orange
3 eggs at room temperature
415 g flour
25 g cocoa powder
2 teaspoons baking powder
pinch of salt
70 g crystallised ginger, chopped into small dice
50 g chocolate chips

Preheat the oven to 180°C. Line a roasting tin with baking parchment.

Cream the butter, sugar and zest together. Add the eggs, one at a time. Stir the flour, cocoa powder, baking powder and salt and add it to the butter and sugar mix. Stir until combined. Add the ginger and chocolate chunks until well distributed. Transfer the dough onto the baking tray and form into a log that is about 30 x 10 cm. Bake for about 25 minutes or until a skewer inserted in the centre comes out clean.

Let the log cool completely and then slice it into ½ cm thick pieces. Place the cookies onto the baking sheet and bake at 160°C for about 10 minutes. Then flip them over and bake for an additional 10–15 minutes or until dry.

# chocolate and oat biscuits

from Trine
makes 32 biscuits

½ cup porridge oats
100 g butter
¼ cup sugar
¾ cup flour
½ teaspoon baking powder
50 g chocolate chips

Trine's children love these cookies.
Enjoy them with a cup of hot milk
and honey.

Preheat the oven to 200°C. Line a baking tray with paper.

Toast the oats until light brown, then let cool. Mix the butter and sugar until pale and fluffy. Add oats, flour and baking powder. Combine well and then gently fold in chocolate chips. Divide into 32 parts and shape into small balls, then use a fork to flatten them slightly.

Bake for 10 minutes, or until dry.

# Measurements I have used

Liquid
1 cup = 250 ml
4 cups = 1 litre

Sugar
1 cup = 220 g
½ cup = 110 g

Flour
1 cup = 150 g
½ cup= 75 g

Wholemeal flour or icing sugar
1 cup = 160 g
½ cup = 80 g

1 tablespoon = 20 ml
1 teaspoon = 5 ml

celsius to fahrenheit
150°C = 300°F
180°C = 350°F
200°C = 375°F

l = litre
ml = millilitre
g = grams
kg = kilogram
C = celsius
F = fahrenheit

THIS IS A BOOK MADE WITH HELP AND LOVE FROM MANY PEOPLE. I ESPECIALLY OWE GRATITUDE TO MY PARTNER ARNSTEIN, MY SISTER MARIA AND, OF COURSE, MY MUM WHO HAS HELPED ME, INSPIRED ME AND DONE ALL THE BEAUTIFUL WORK ON THE LAY-OUT. THANKS TO ALL MY CONTRIBUTORS FOR SHARING THEIR RECIPES. THANKS ALSO TO EVA AND TORIL FOR LETTING ME BORROW THEIR TREASURES FOR MY PHOTOS. THE UNIQUE RETRO CUPS AND PLATES HAVE GIVEN